To all the beautiful people in life

who have made my frustrations all possible. From the gazilion boyfriends to all the dads that claimed my blood....

To the beauties of the present who saved my life and allowed me to heal while pursing their lips.

The ones who stuck by my side and never avoided me because i was just too

real
raw
weird
honest
immoral
whatever

and once i healed, forced me to organize these books after years of creating.

thank you thank you thank you thank you thank you thank you thank you thank you.

The greatest appreciation goes out to my mentors.

Gordon , Nancy and Neal, Kristina, Todrick, and Pele

ha ha ha

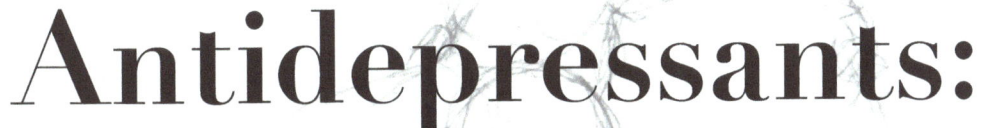

Antidepressants:

explosions from a frustrated mind

volume#1

Sophia Leah

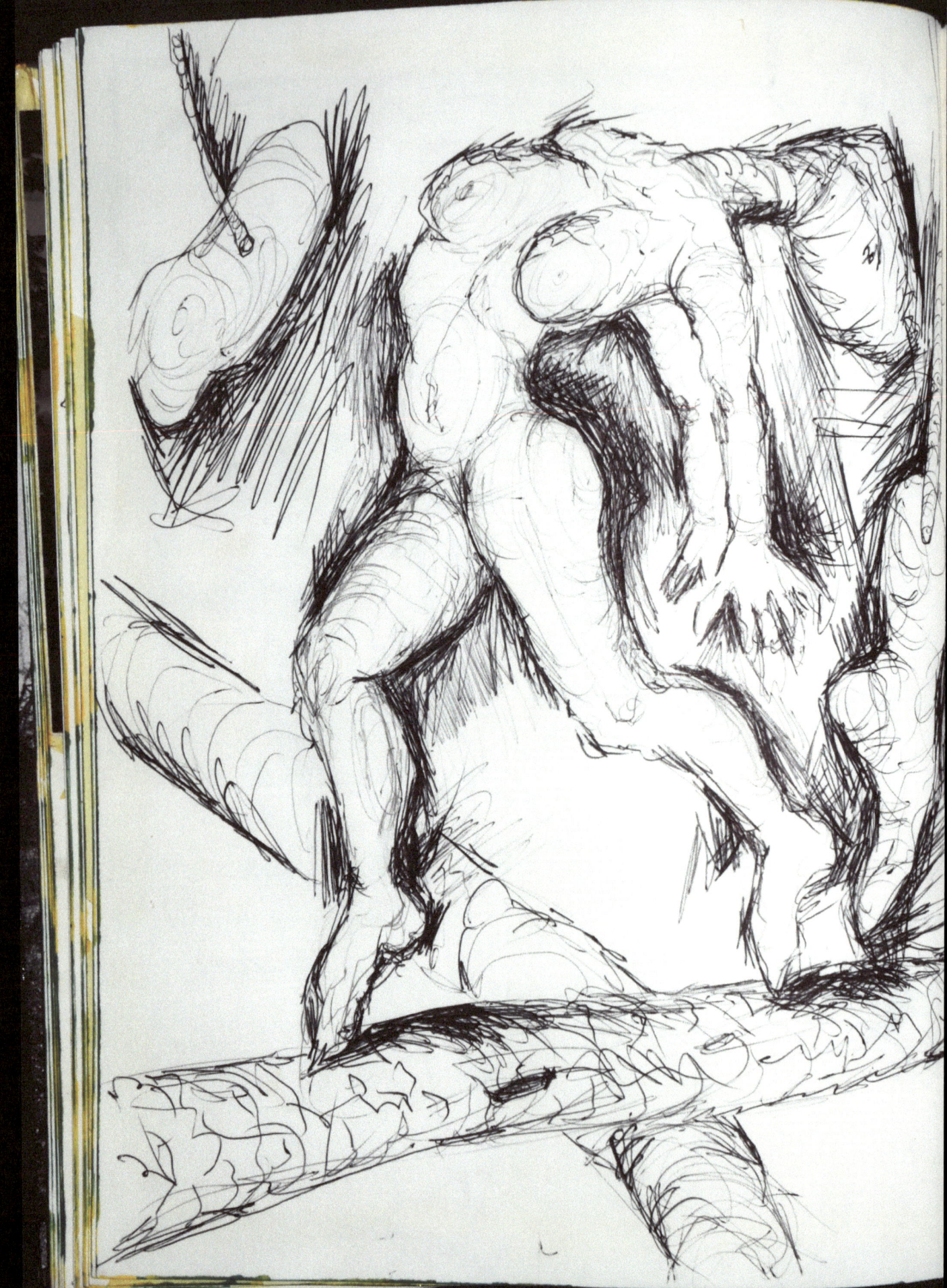

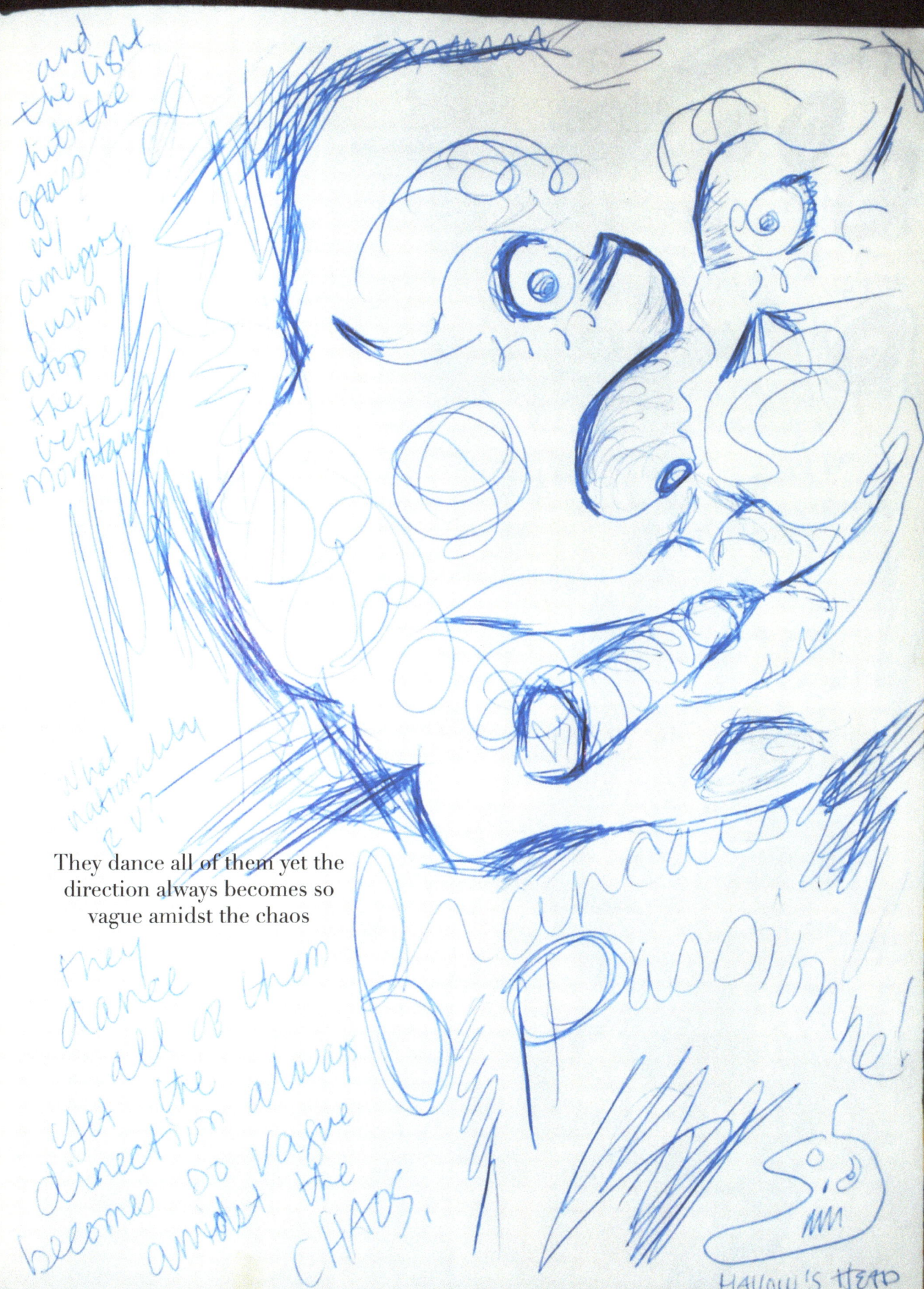

They dance all of them yet the
direction always becomes so
vague amidst the chaos

My mind is aware yet stands still in the chaos.

Words can't express it...then I findy myself giving up.

Am I REALLY saying nothing?

They grow stronger within that subconscious. The lines are always shown amidst the chaos into infinity.

What is real beyond our existence?

I always feel like crying.....

it's the date

my mind is aware yet stands still in the chaos.

WORDS CAN'T EXPRESS it...Then I find myself giving up

"fill the room trying to find the you always sleep, yet the words TALK in your sleep, yet the words are nothing yet your speak so Clearly."

I have a feeling mad

What is real beyond our existence

What is my ___?

I always feel like crying

So Am I Really saying nothing

they glow still longer
within in
that
siberon's
gios

the lines
are always
shown amidst

the
purple chaos
into infinity

Remember in your thoughts

it will come along and must.

you dont want to know what day it is.

its striking you that the day is more important than you think

maybe nothing is more important than the self

a car speeding slowly alone down a street by itself.

Did you see the wonder?

Elements of change searing the path.

Paint it green.

Calm down your neurotic piece of flesh

as if i am not crazy enough.

Its killing me. Killing fields.

Down with it all.

The Earth must stand and fight!

remembering in your
thoughts that it will
come along and must
Because you don't want to
know what day it is, but it
keep striking you-that perhaps
the day is more important
that you think Maybe
nothing is more important
than the Self actually alone
as a car speeding down
alone down a street by itself
Did you see the wonder
Elements of change bearing the
path.
        Paint it green.
                Fime your smile
calm down you neurotic peine
                flesh As if I'm
not crazy enough alone
Its killing me
        killing fields
Down with it all!
        The Earth must
stand + fight!!

go what
oB you
Brian

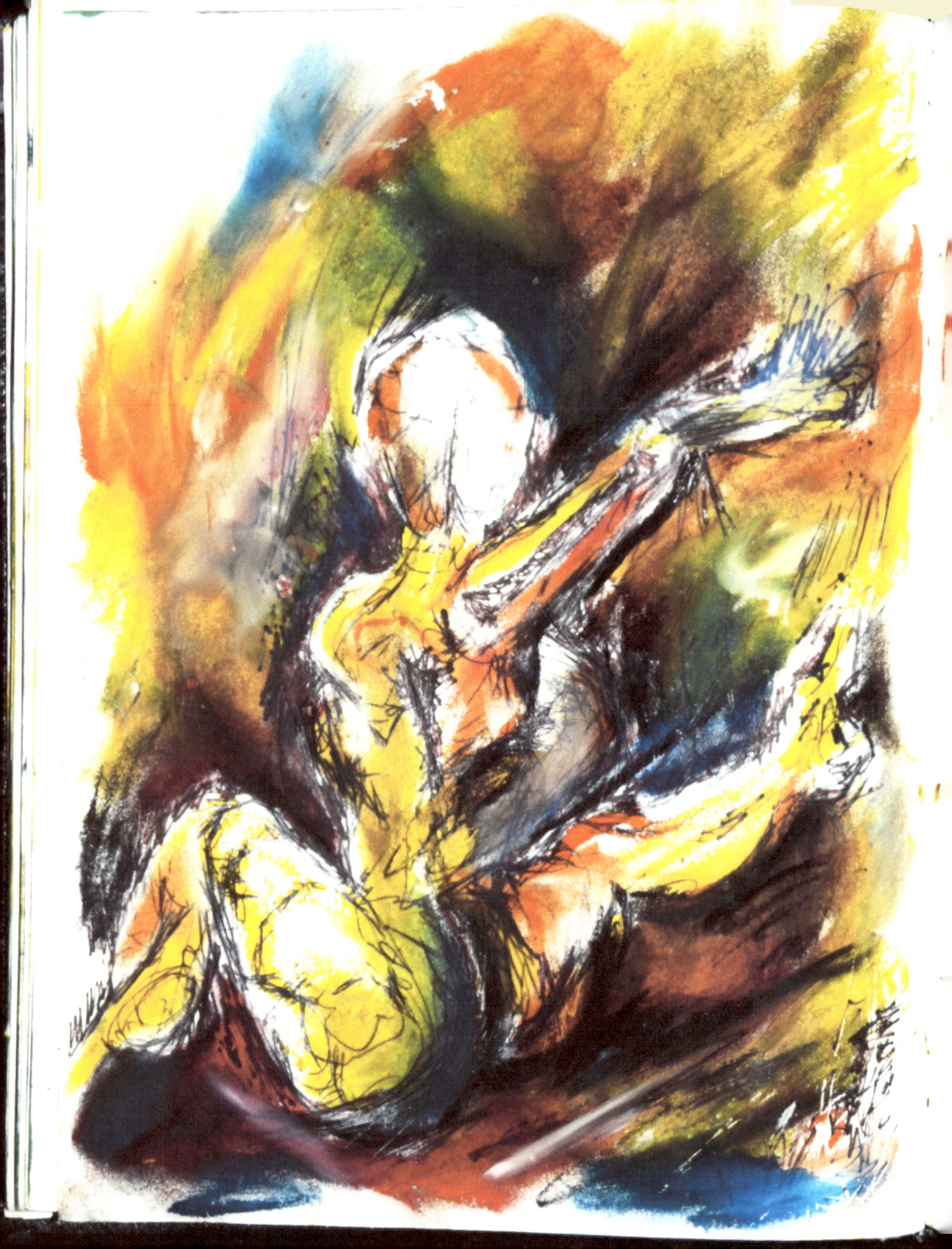

Denise was working on
inside a large, arched structure
applying a final dabs of brown
paint to it and humming abstractedly
to the Cocteau twins - like some
bizarre postmodern canary.

Denise smeared paint across her
forehead with the back of her hand
and blinked at her cage.

JILL

○

HELEN! I HAVE A simple
life: I get up, I go to the
work pub. Sometimes I go to the pub
sometimes when your not having one
of your black fits, I see you. You're
right. I don't understand you. You're
here. You go to classes. You see me.

" Why do you have to
complicate your life
so much?

BIZARRE POSTMODERN CANARY.

You frollic with joy it kills to experience. None. NO! NOT A BIG HEAD. Alcoholic stop shit health bullshit Jesus. Why? As if it matters AND then insecurity kills the heart.

All I want is an A a big LARGE mini world that I can stuff my brains compactly into.

hide em out, yet savor them alone pour them out into this world of conflict. A Free Museum WONDERFUL!.

_____

Paintings w/Dirt, leaves.
            brown pebbles.
                  goopy green Sea.
                        leave
      mixed w/ Acrylic.

You frollic with joy
it kills to experience more. NO!
Not a BIG HEAD
Alcoholic Stop Shit health bullshit Jesus.
Why?
As if it Matters.
And Then Insecurity kills
the heart.

IT's

"She does strange things
to planes

All I Want is a big large
Mini world I can Stuff my brains
compactly into.
hide 'em out, yet savor them
and pour them
out
into this world of conflict.

Paintings with dirt, leaves, brown pebbles, Goopy green Sea

DO

WORDS EXPLAIN

the Space

Les

IT's LOST
her voice
yesteryear
it ran behind the
to see

I SAT
    I in my room. Always alone, always
So Isolated   dazed + confused.
                    We keep
on going of the
                    changes

they
don't
stop

my

then I remember that
sunset cityscapes

BORDERLINE

so

6

"Ticket please

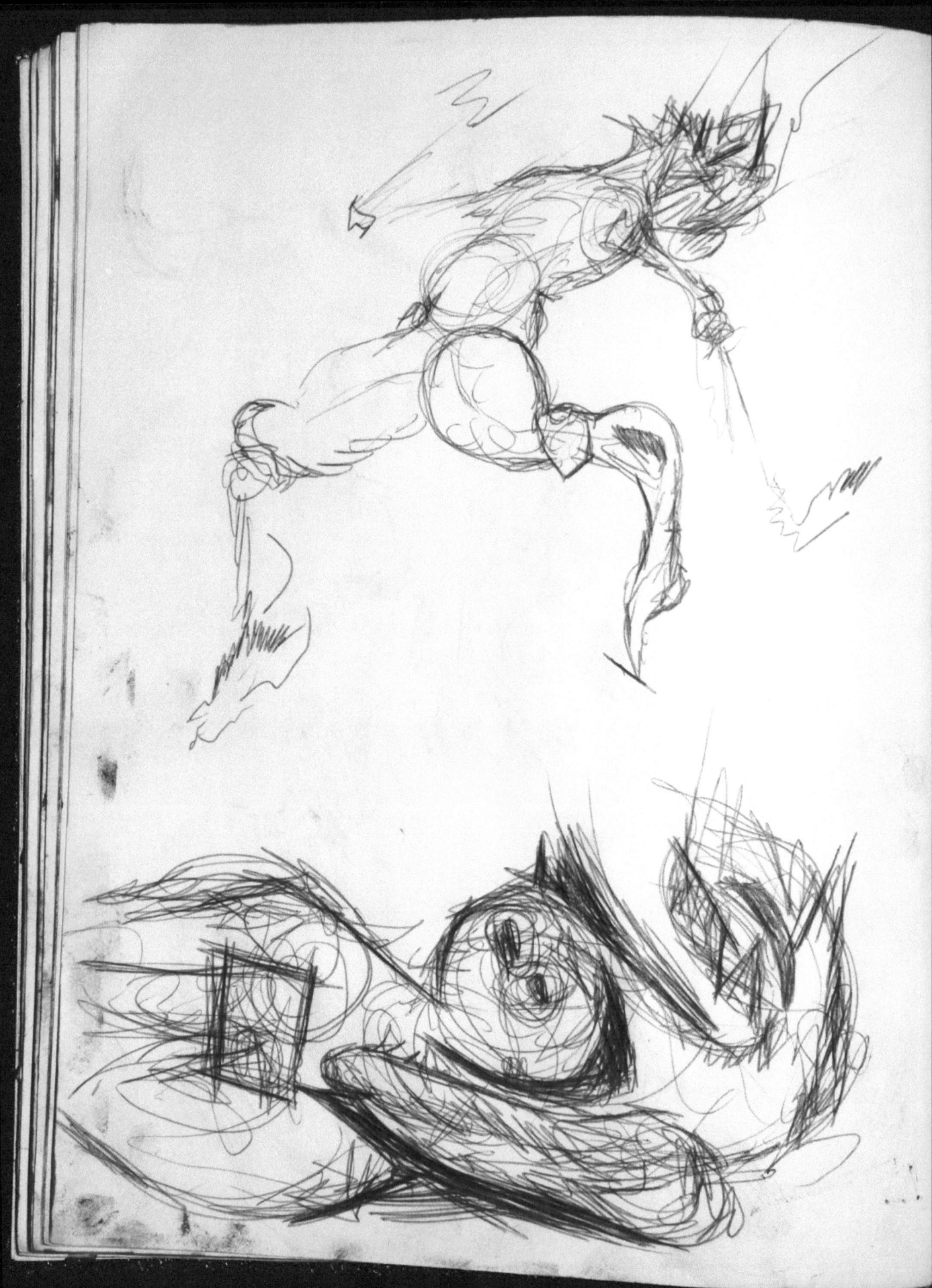

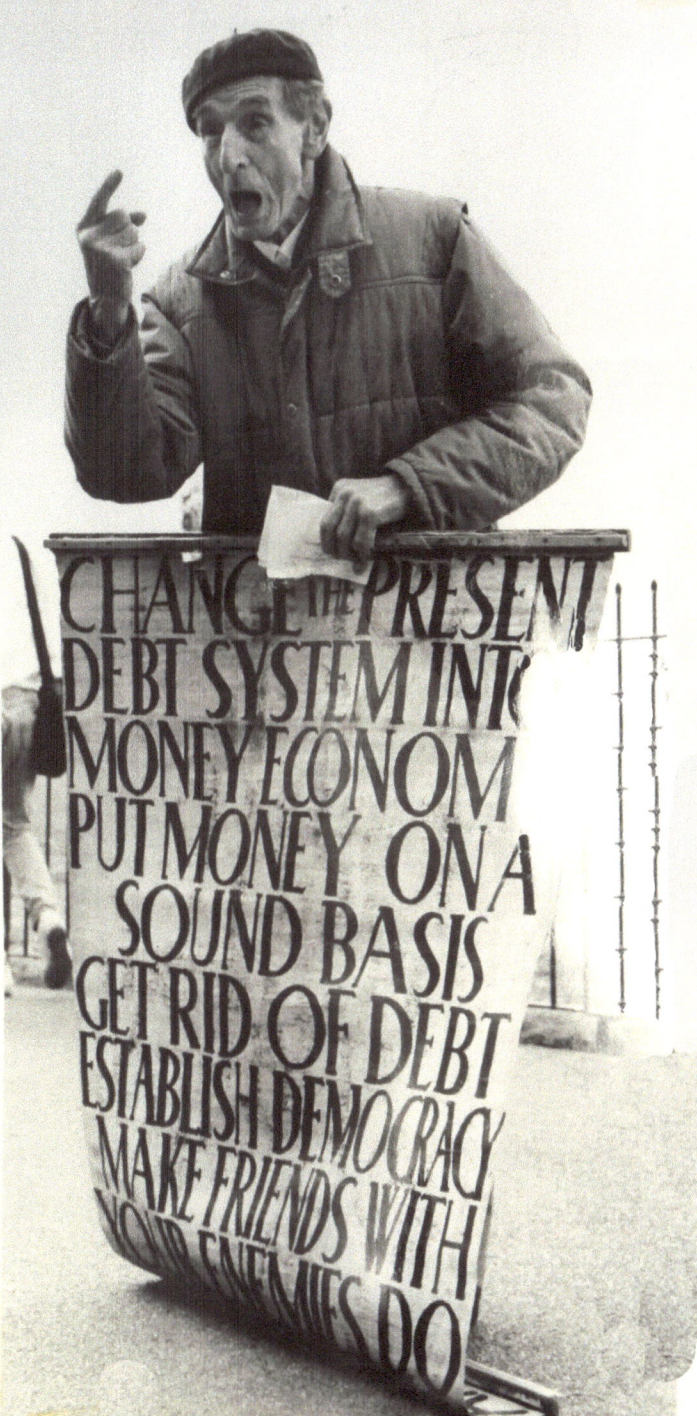

Missy - what ya doin'

pooin'

It goes through the little intestine and pushes through

leave my books alone

Run Away. Run Away.

Hide behind the willow tree. world.

She was so upset

she ran away crying

The fruit flies tickles her toes while she ran.
She was so upset she

ran away crying.

What do you need now darling?

Sweet

Lady of Love

I will be running

amidst city streets,
buzzing lights,
flickering souls creating the

essence of
intensity.

Loving it
always Needing
input

cities give you
information to dance
freely.

Always seeking another. Many resources finding them
never is a problem.
WRONG.

My family's
relationship has finally developed into a pleasant one.

I intrude upon
their domain
and it plagues me with illness.

A love affair of distance always seems to fly.

NEVER THROW UP
ON YOUR LOVER

#67

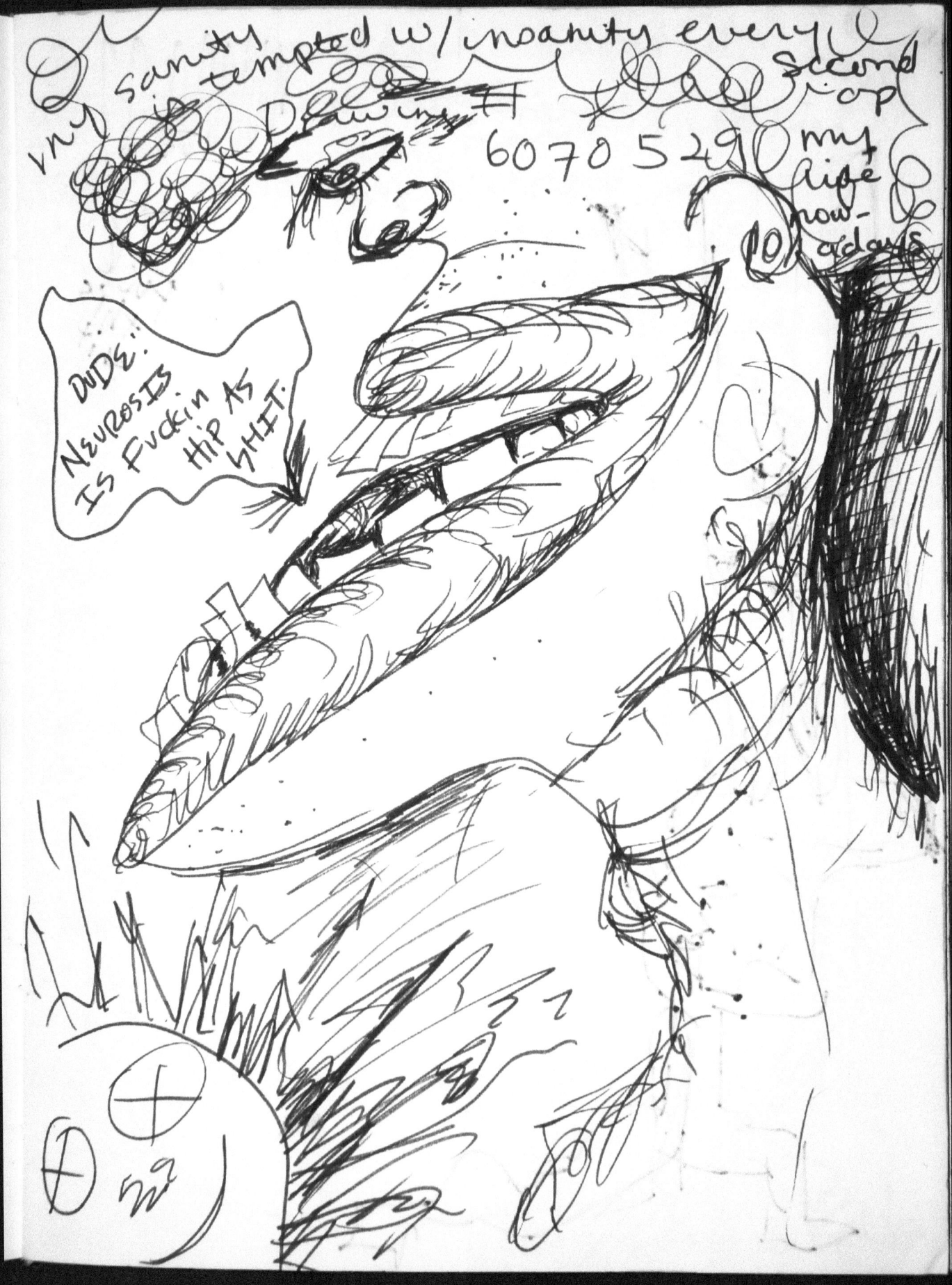

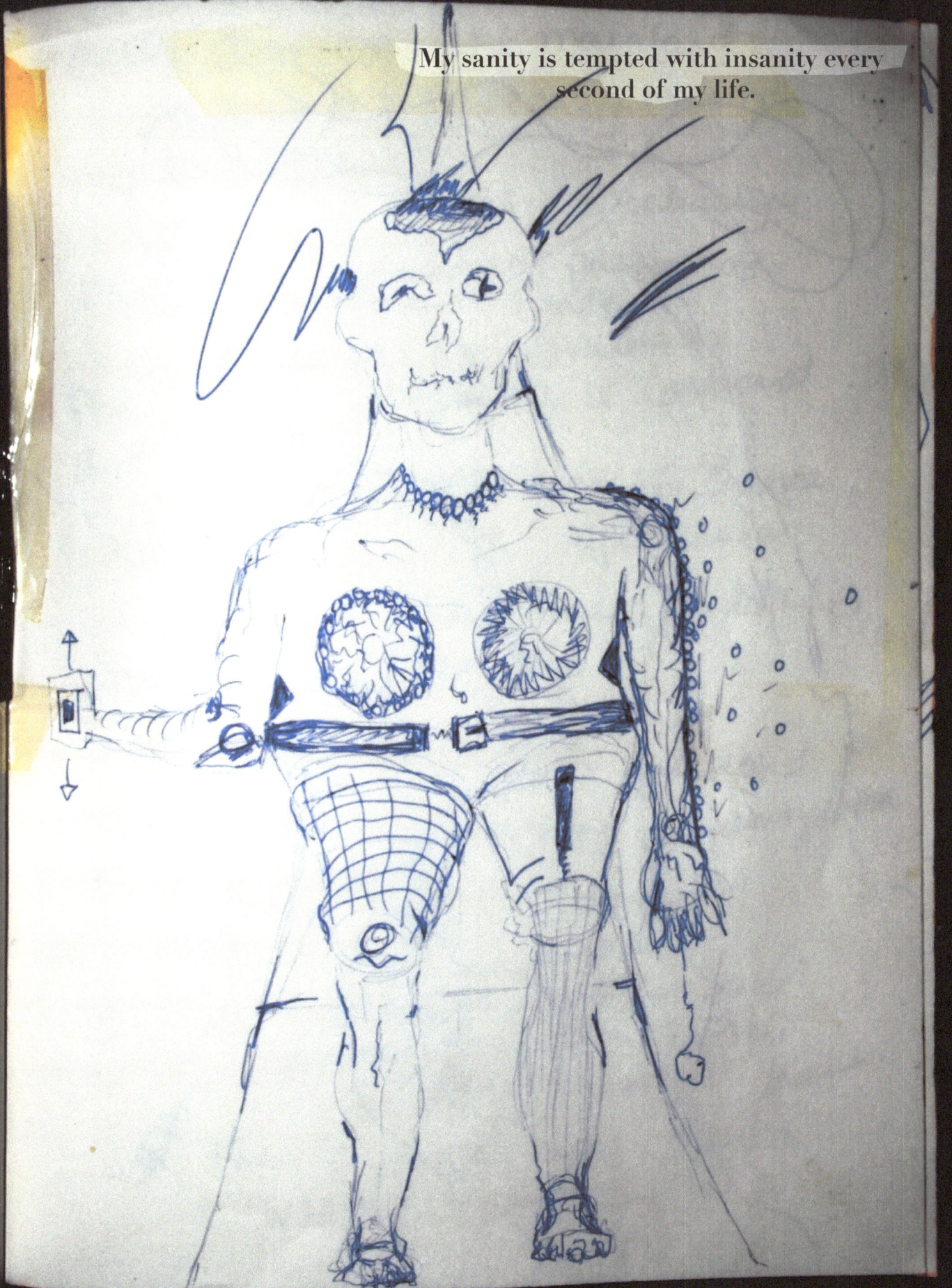

daddy #3

- GOT YOUR LETTER AND WAS EAGER FOR MORE NEWS SO I CALLED NANCY LAST NITE. SEND ME A POST-CARD FROM BANGKOK + DO!! WRITE FROM KENYA IMMED. HAVE BEEN OBSESSIVELY PREOCCUPIED WITH MY OWN SITUATION OR I OBVIOUSLY WOULD HAVE WRITTEN... BUT I THINK OF YOU EVERY DAY... MY PROBLEM IS THAT ON 8/1 I PAINTED THOSE ② 4'x6' PAINTINGS I LIKE SO MUCH + ITS BEEN DRIVING ME CRAZY. OH... I SOLD 27 REMAINING PAINTINGS TO SOME GUY FROM VIENNA. LOVE DAD

Dear Sophia

Got your letter and was eager for more news so I called Nancy last nite. Send me a post card from Bangkok and do!! Write from Kenya Immediately. Have been obsessively preoccupied with my own situation or I obviously would have written... But I think of you every day...my problem is that on August first I painted those two 4 by 6 paintings I like so much and its been driving me crazy. OH...I sold 27 of the remaining paintings to some guy from Vienna.

LOVE DAD

Daddy + mommy equal kid called child

Is it me?

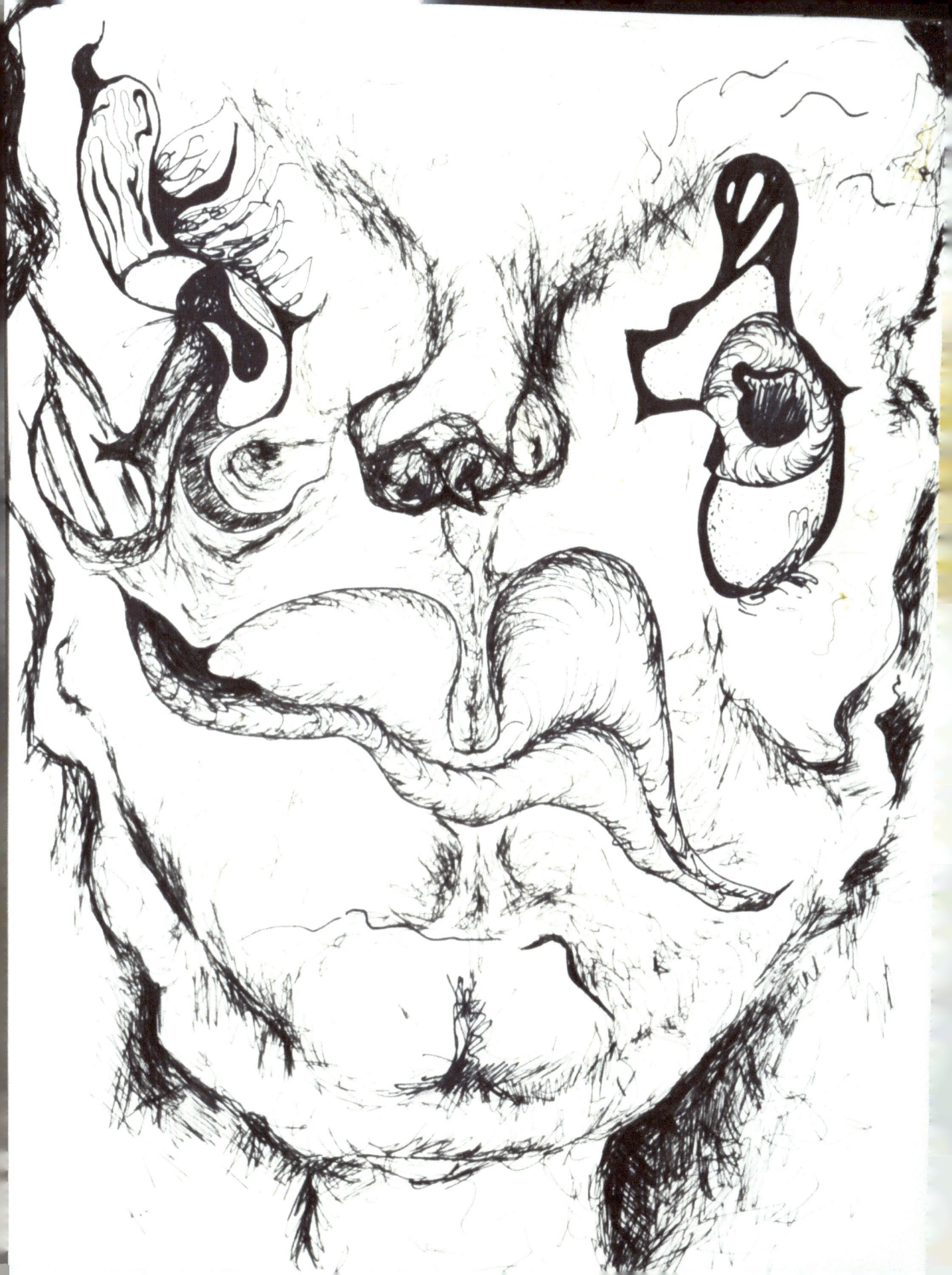

I feel fat right now. Ive gained weight from drinking so damn much.
It was last night. I'll just fast tomorrow.....
so I dont feel like an immense blubbery mass. Drinking
makes you massive. GOD-infatuation with weight...I HAVE TO be so conscious of it.

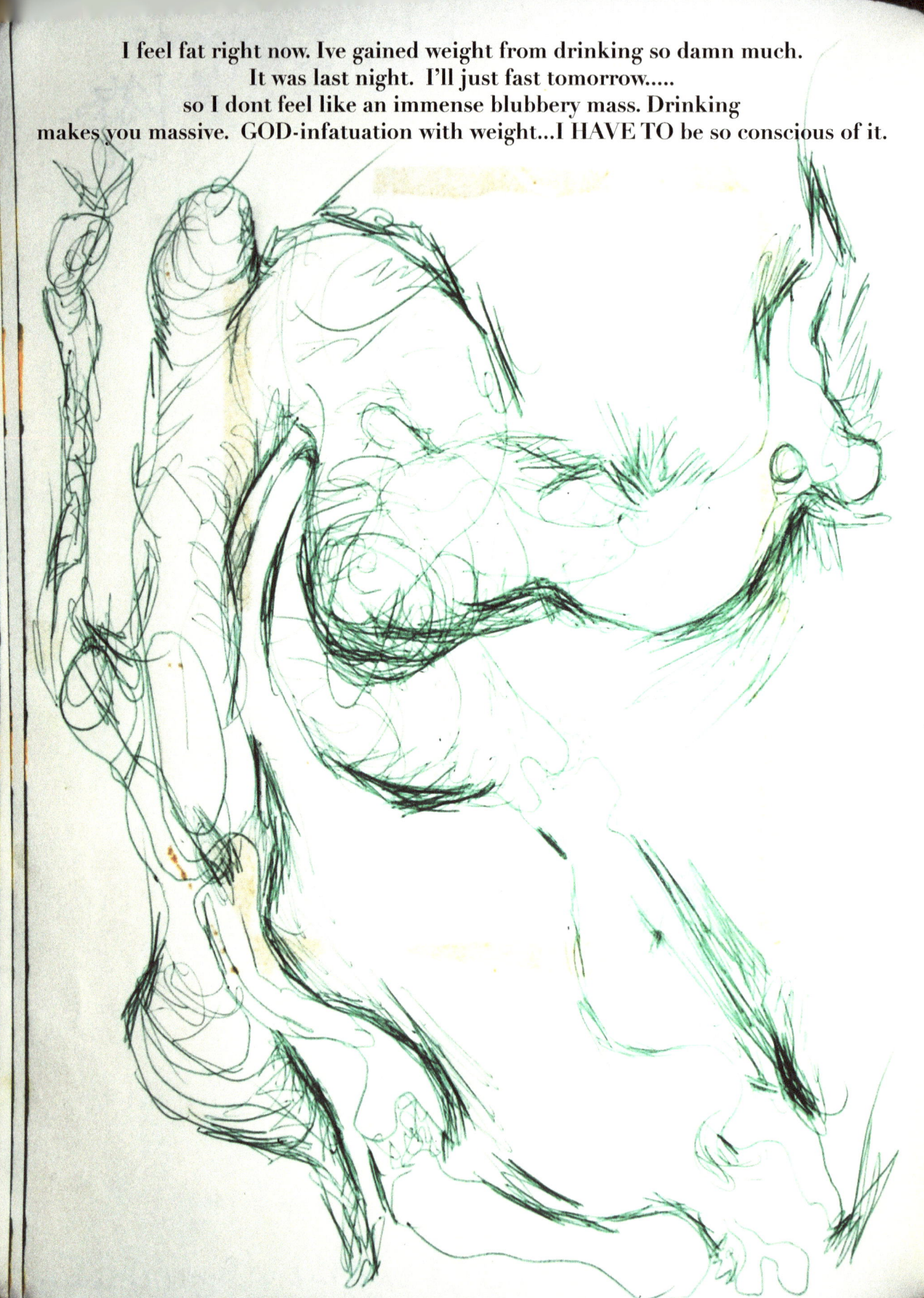

I feel very fat right now — I'm sure I've gained a bit op wait from drinking so Damn much. It was last night — I'll just fast tomorrow — So I don't feel like I'm an immense disgusting blubbery mass of fat. Eating is healthy, but drinking makes you gain massive + fast.

GOD — Infatuation with Wright. Yet I have to be so conscious of it.

Dont let it die.
Heather its dying.

Earth decays like life and
words from human flesh.

Religion thru bullshit
description.

Piss me off.

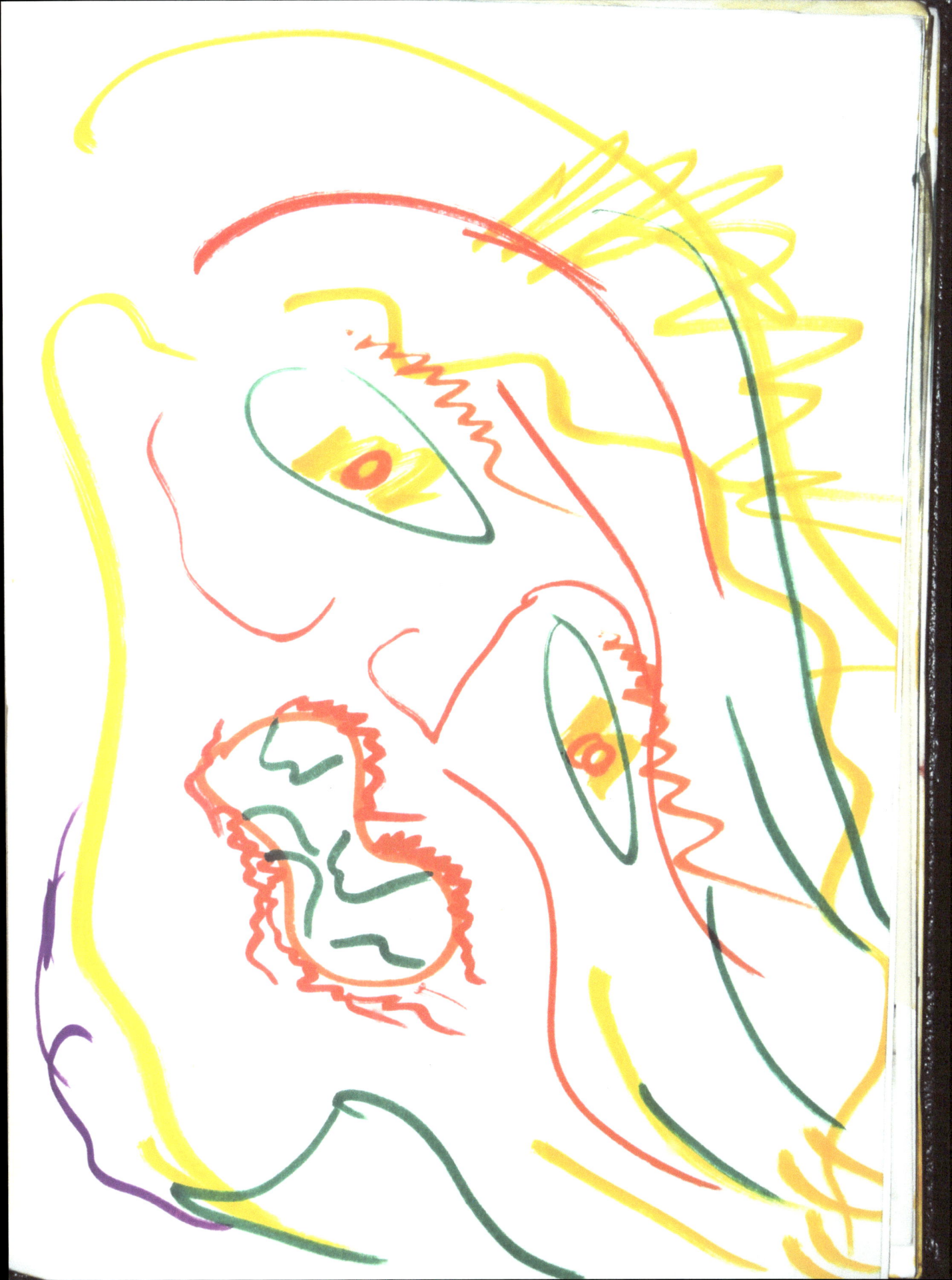

It's ... ... when you

Stay ... ...

da... around ... ...

Everything spinning

... ... when you're at

night ... ...

... ... thinking about ...

Roya... hotel and chilly London

flat ... #6 ma... ...ue. (with an E)

wondering if it really was (answer

London ... ... resume me.

... ... Who Am Me?

Who ... ... Florence flashbacks

my brain shuffles through

these quickly passing days

shooting time like a breath

of gold.

chilly gold, cold windows and

talking in my sleep.

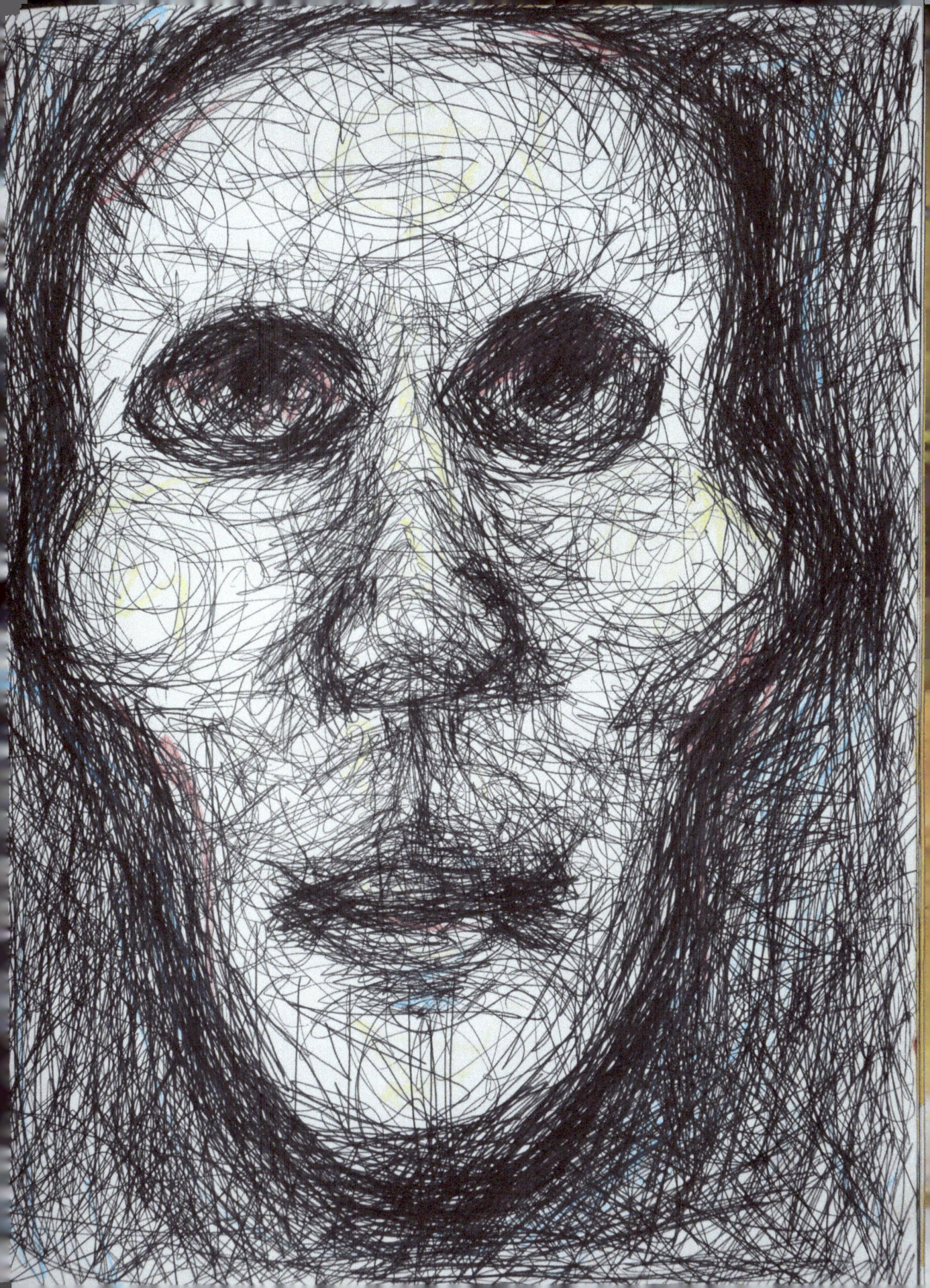

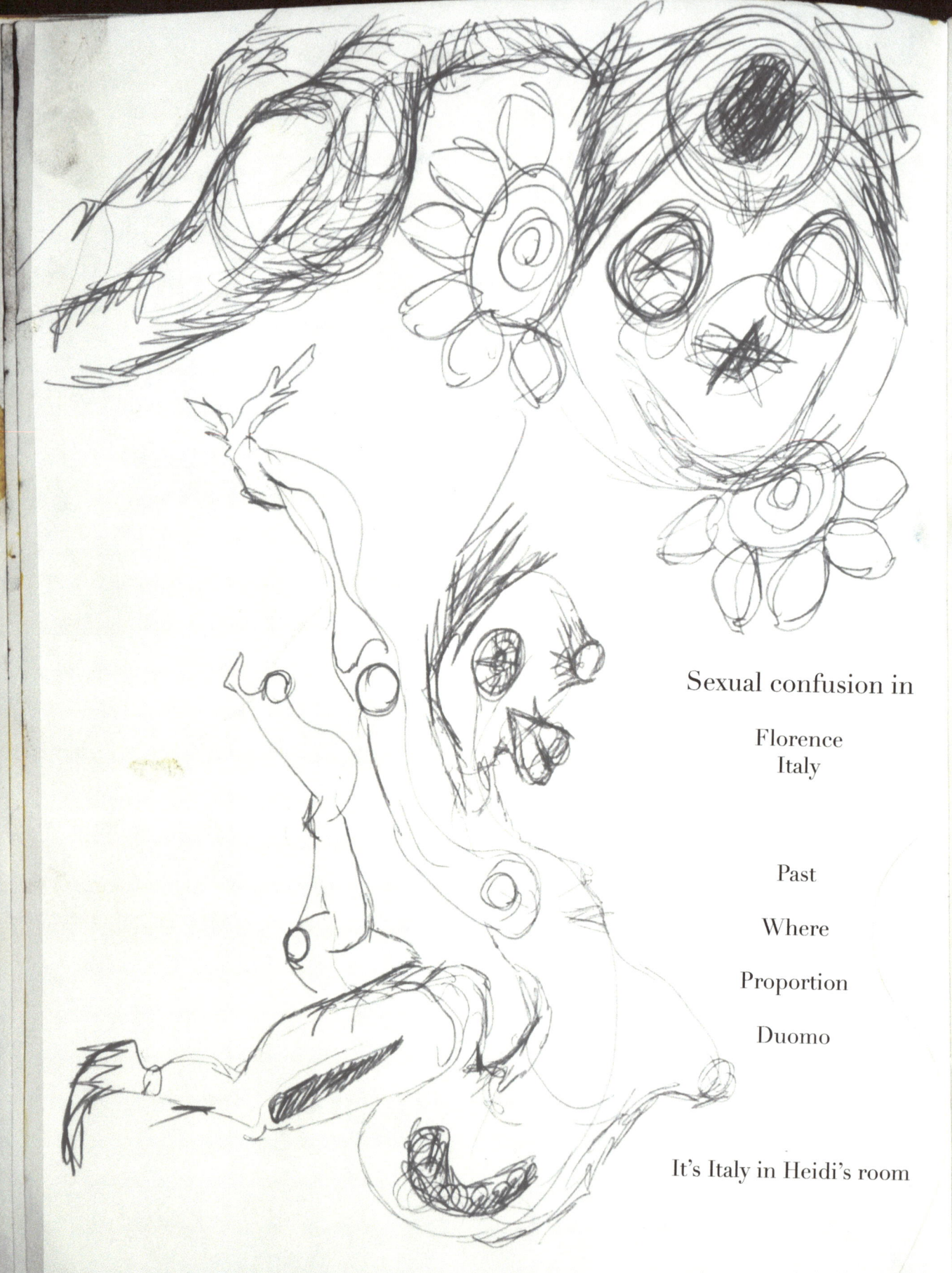

Sexual confusion in

Florence
Italy

Past

Where

Proportion

Duomo

It's Italy in Heidi's room

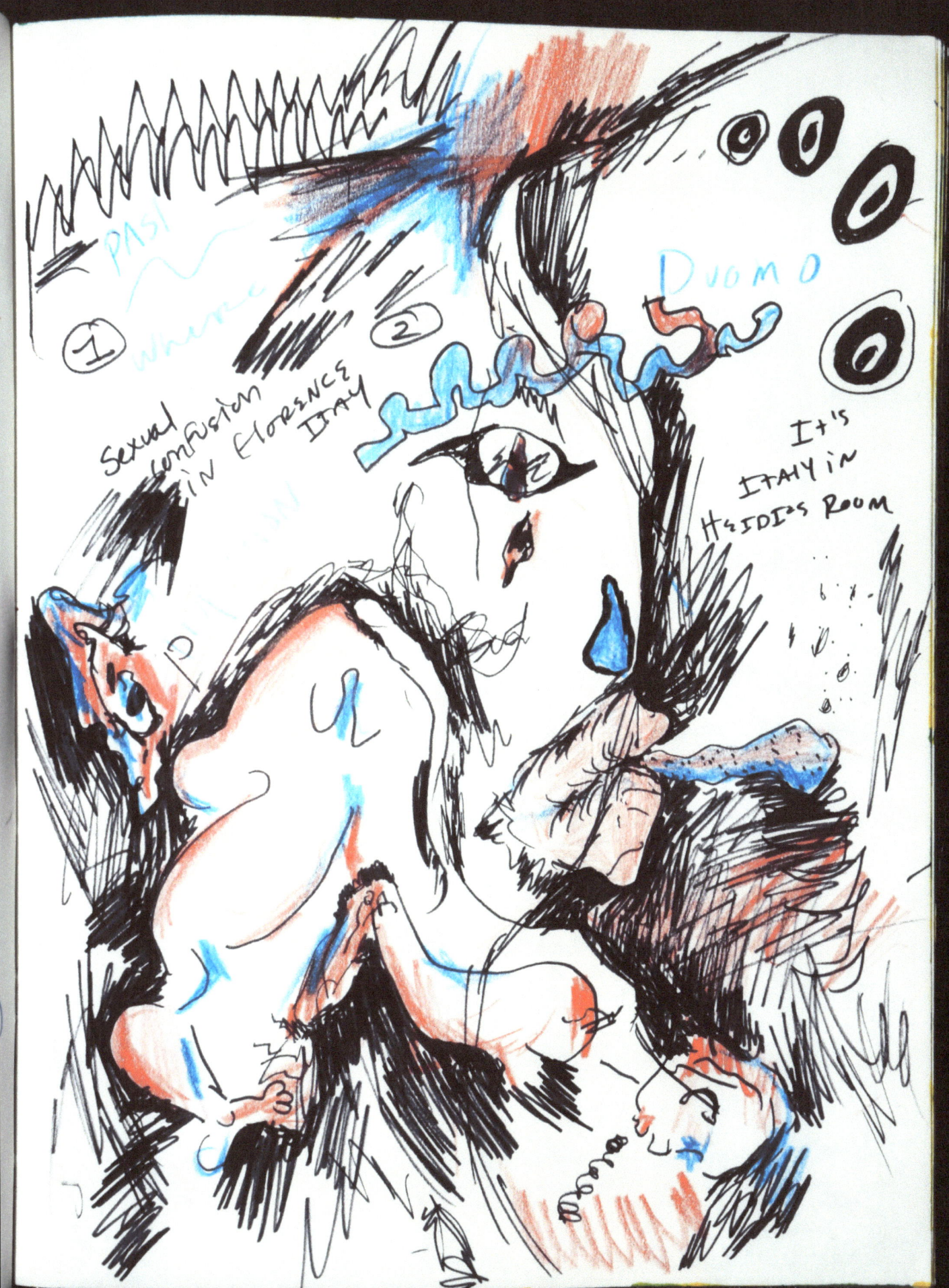

The whole a
concept was a
"dualism" As all life forms
perform with a sense Of And
destiny routine purpose life
what to do with the questioned,
alotted that destiny is created. + formed
of another book
a confusing relapse hiberation occurs.
crumbling out.

The girl
Screamed
As the dog
Chewed her eyeballs
into bloody welts of
mutilated mesh. It was
a huge sight.
He wanted a
drink. fragment of coffee to
out of a tube
of plastic

perhaps it
WAS ONLY
then that the Story no 7-11 store.
Contained itself.
BIGGULPSHIT.
What WASHe to do.

AND DAVID'S
SOUL SCREAMED OUT LOUD IN
VIVISECTION.

The whole concept is a dualism

as all life forms perform with a sense of destiny and routine
purpose.

What to do with the life allotted is the question.

A best is created, formed.

A confusing relapse.

then hibernation occurs

thrusting out.

"SUBTANCE ABUSE"

"self indulgent
bullshit"

I fucking

love it!

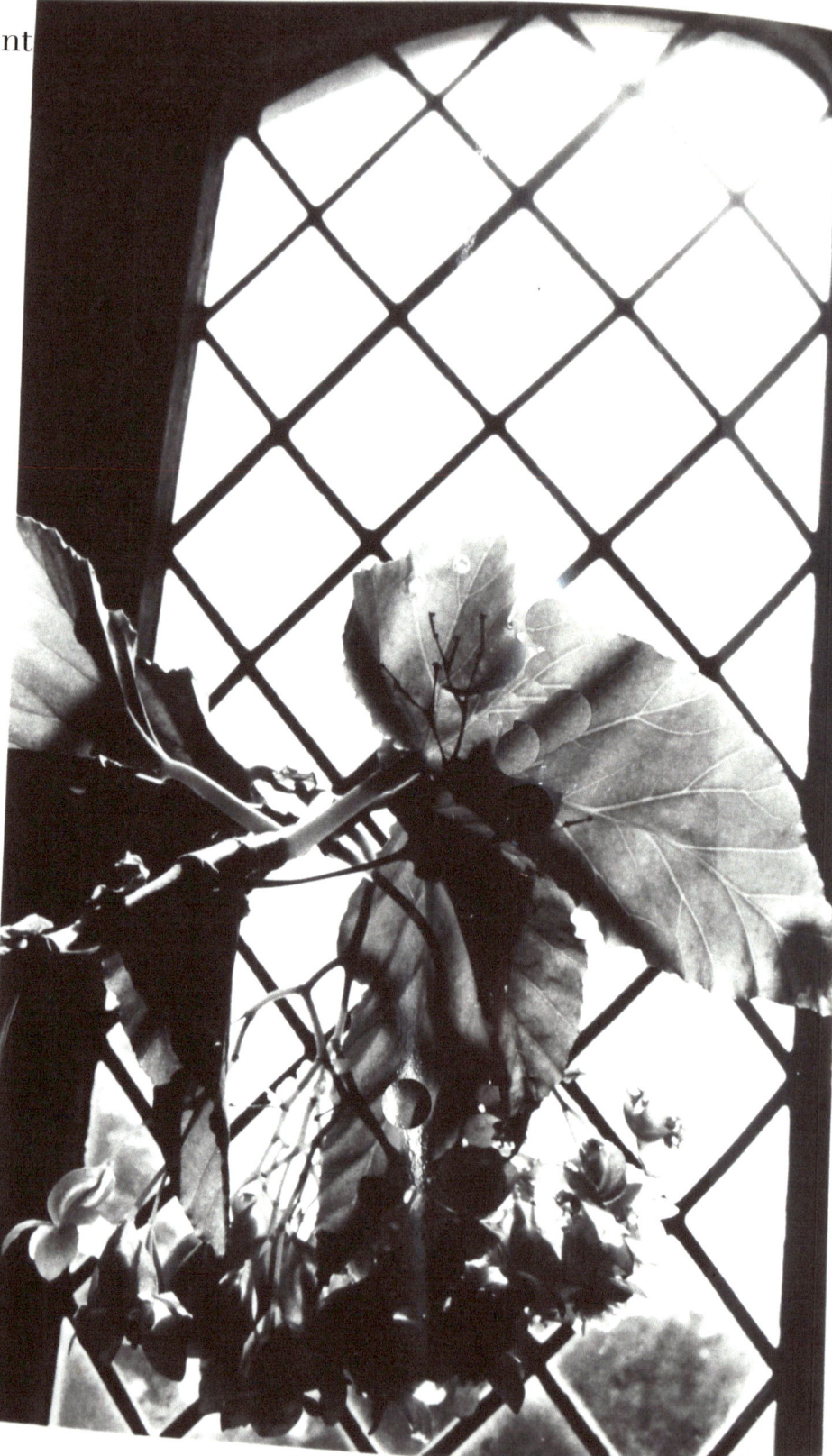

I fucking
Like.... go....
love it.

"self indulgent
bullshit" TONY
SAYS!

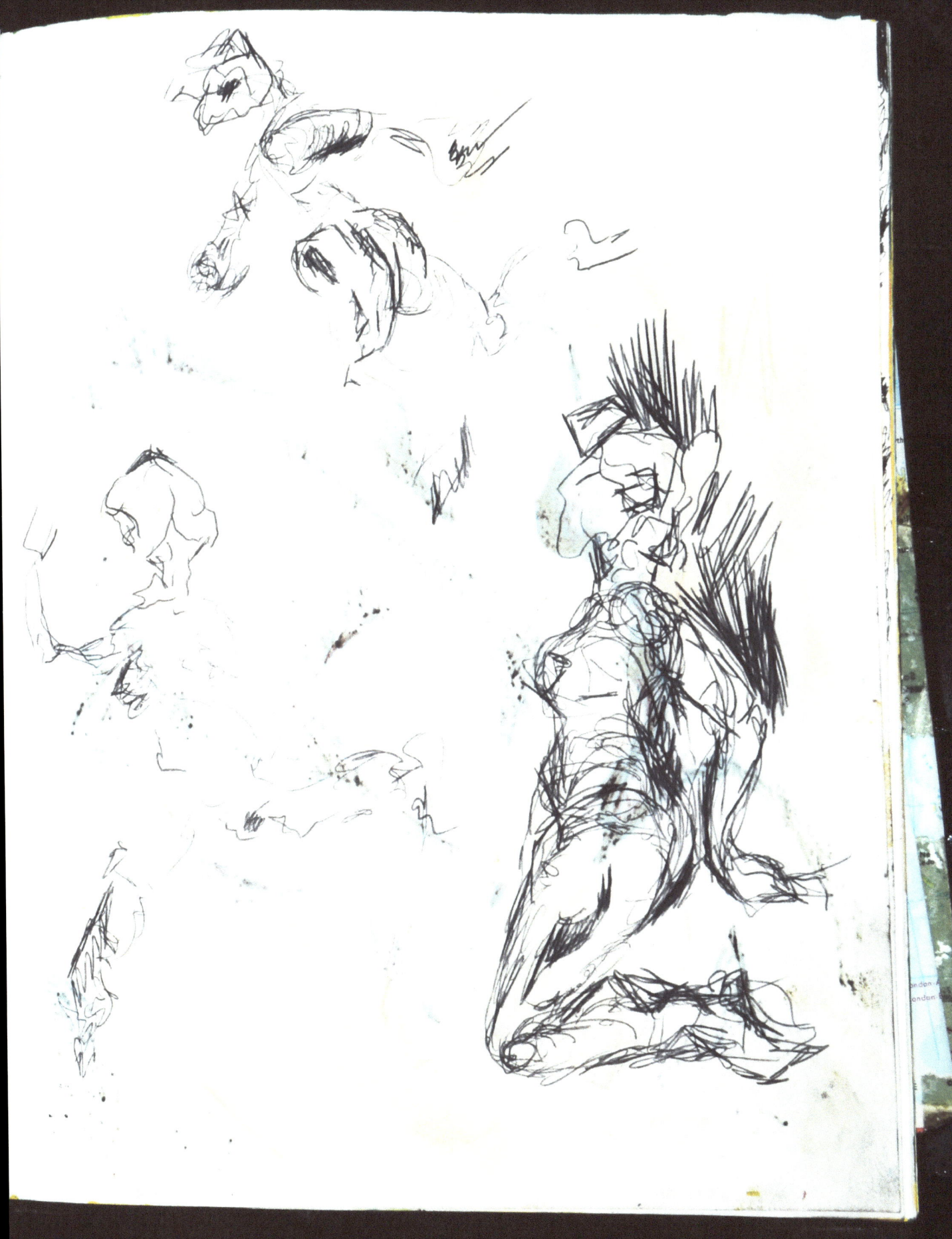

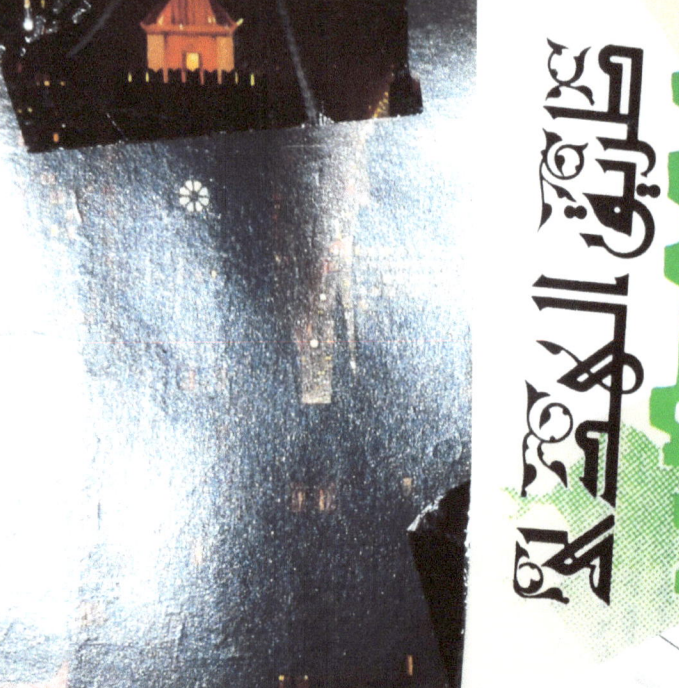

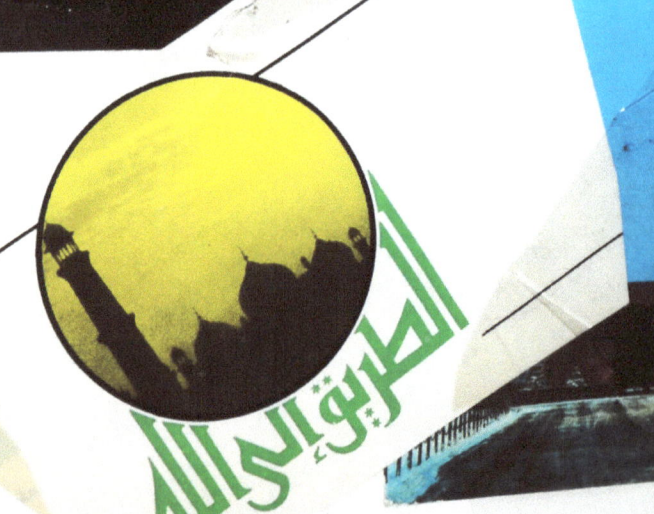

الحربية السودانية

الطيران السوداني

I want my

Boogie

with the electricity

to be covered

SALEM
KEIZER

Chadwick
Corner

WALLACE

I want my body

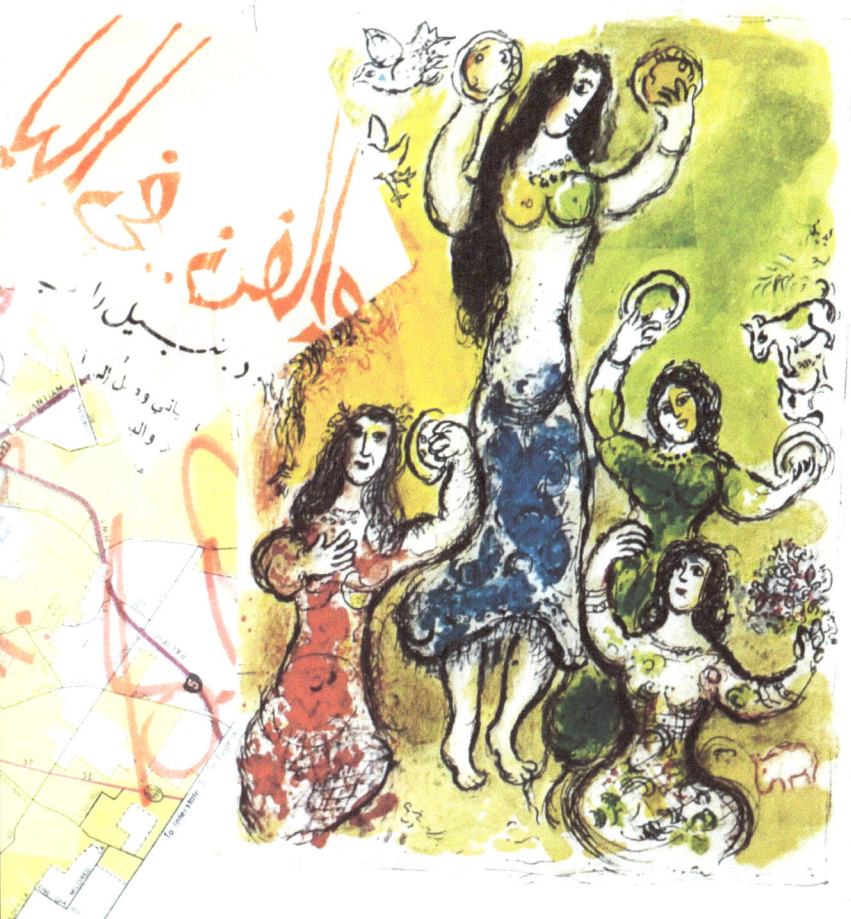

to be covered

with wisps of your hair.

so everywhere i go

will be as beautiful

All the lost boysies flailing around

young bloods to suck from my internal struggle.

Flower Petals
Fuck you blond shit hole

Its when your soul gets lost that you feel so depleted mesmerized by
captivating sand flowers

<negative BEING>

I hope these energies don't eat me up and make me die or do they
strengthen my

sense of
existence?

Inertia soul floats.

In a week she will be in New York then she goes to London,

then shed an inner
lining and scream in pain.

squelching and belching

Flower
Petals

Fuck you
BLOND SHIT
HOLE.

9-23-90

Kenya
almost
DONE

Its   When your soul
gets lost that you feel so depleted -
mesmerized by captivating sand
                                Flowers

I hope these
energies don't eat me
up + make me die or
do they
strengthen
my sense   INERTIA
of existence?   SOUL   {negative}
                         {BEING.}
                    FLOAT

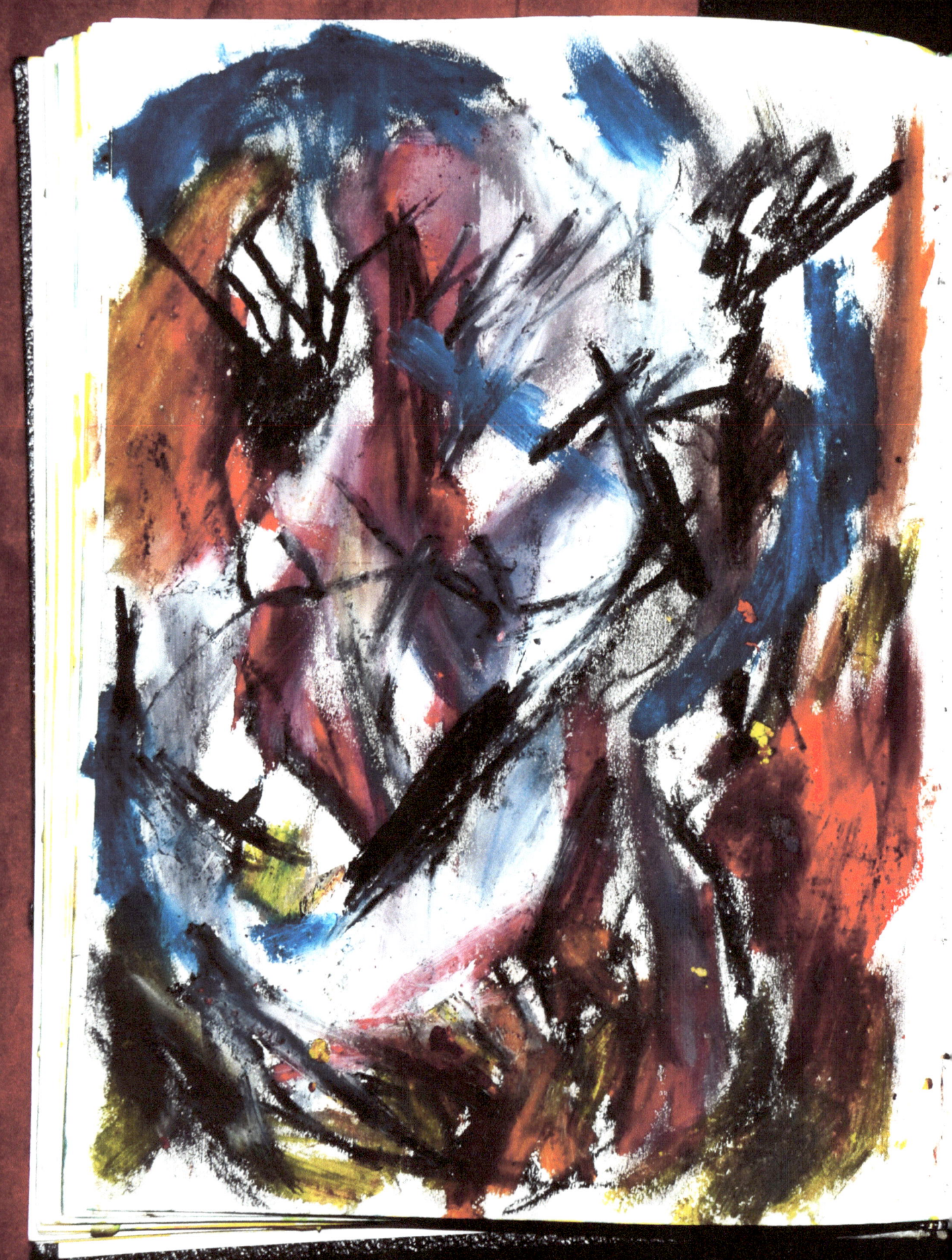

HIGH STREET KENSINGTON

The SQUARE WAS SO BOLD
~The WALLS within it so thick
                reaching the realms
    So close yet running
                    always
                        Away

ticking, ticking
        Bugs Again FLYING IN
                        STRAIGHT
                            LINES

        calling out to mother

all becomes Silent so quick
                        URGH The torment
        of only language
    the letters tones diffuse if that
                the truth.
                        Depletes its
            strength through other
  of untimelyution.   REALMS

pages   pages   pages
         city Fly iN GO By+ you see the

                    proud to be
                        who you
                            ARE

        Isn't so proud
                    to WALK in straight
lines
        OH please eat my ticket up
and let me pass through your
                metallic existence
        let me caress your lonely
                            SCANNER
                    with human love.
     so revealing. Passing by, The light
                        so blue like your
            blinket
                    it TURNS me ON YOUR
     shiny silver Ring like existence.
            RUN my finger through
                    and the cold harshness
of your flesh succumbs to my desires
        OH PASSIONATE WONDER.

trotting through amorphous blob.
amorphous blob trot through
small molecule in this
existence.
GROWTH OF A cell splitting.
Yet so similiar.

Attracting atoms. Ions of attraction
Big Bang.

Let this magnetic force
retract attract Resent its
own Kind?
molecules coincide Knocking
through bubbly
MAzes of confrontational
magnetic fields.

Schism. Fizz

It Flows. Clogging rarely
occurs.
When it does mutancy occurs
and is put to
Death.

Kill it.

ENTER my
Spirit

come
to me + bless me please whatever it is
give me my day fulfill me.
tempting me with
desire and pulling it away.
the reclusive shell I'm being stuck
with
LET ME KNOW THE MEANING!
Give me fulfillment.
tell me
where this power lies.
how to let it come out.
Stuck in this head.
possession.
it's let me scream it to the world.
unsurpassed w/ me. TORTURE
Builds from not having
the outlet. It's not
the mathematic
equation.
it squeeks out in itzy
bitsys.
Jesus! fuck why that word?
small little things I can see it coming.
cherish them. love them
Give them flowers. kiss them +

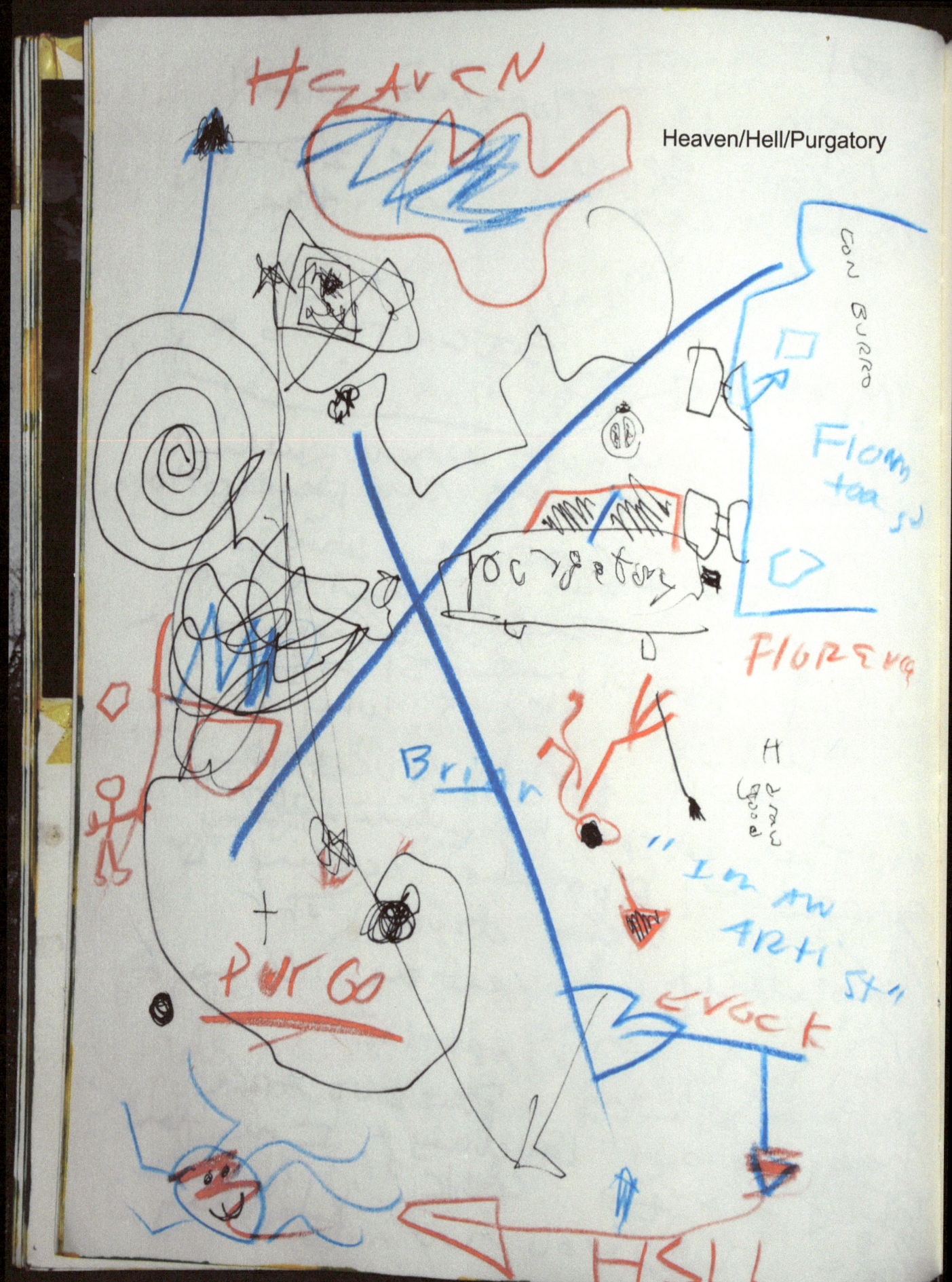

"Going to Bangkok to shop!"

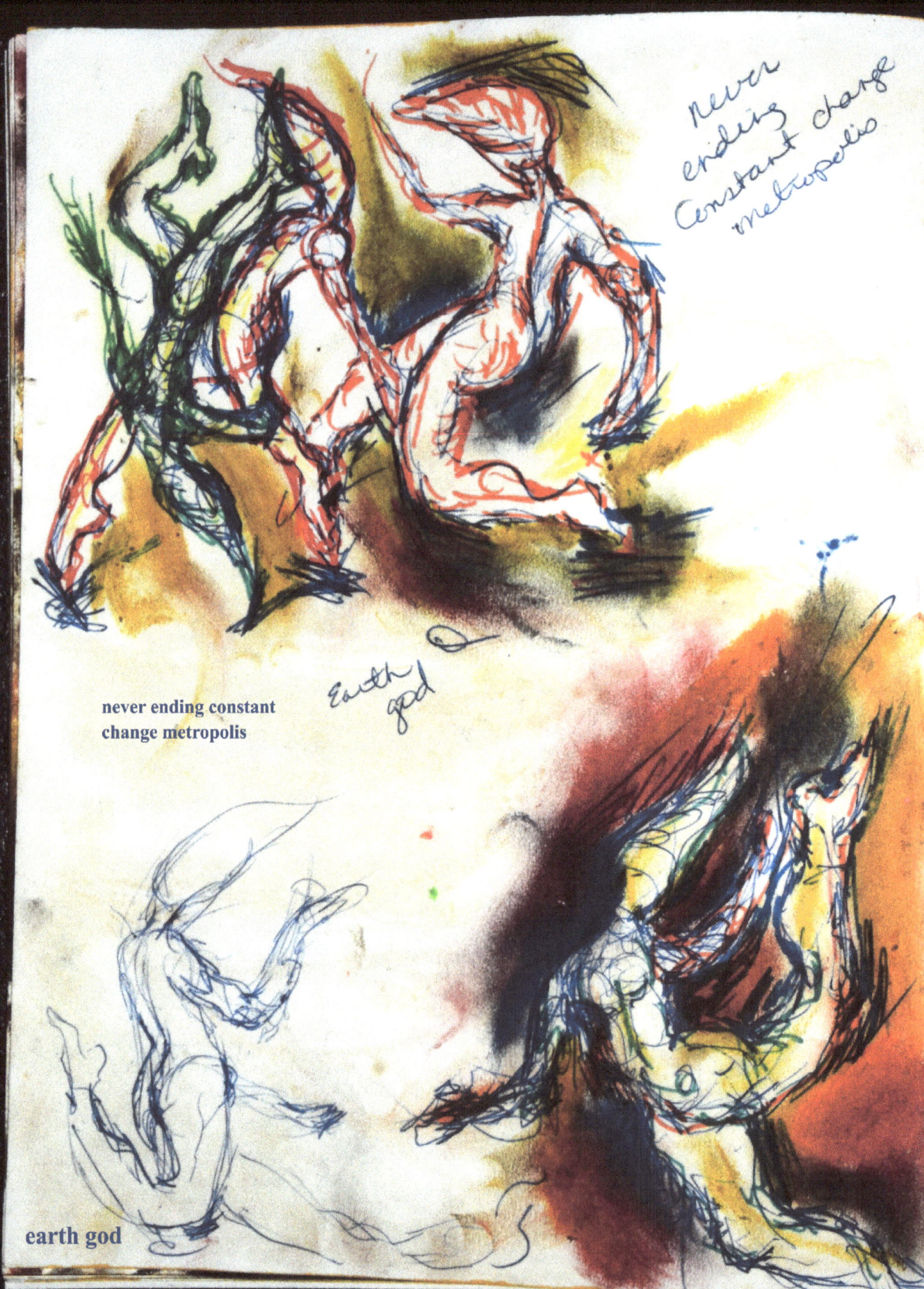

never ending constant
change metropolis

earth god

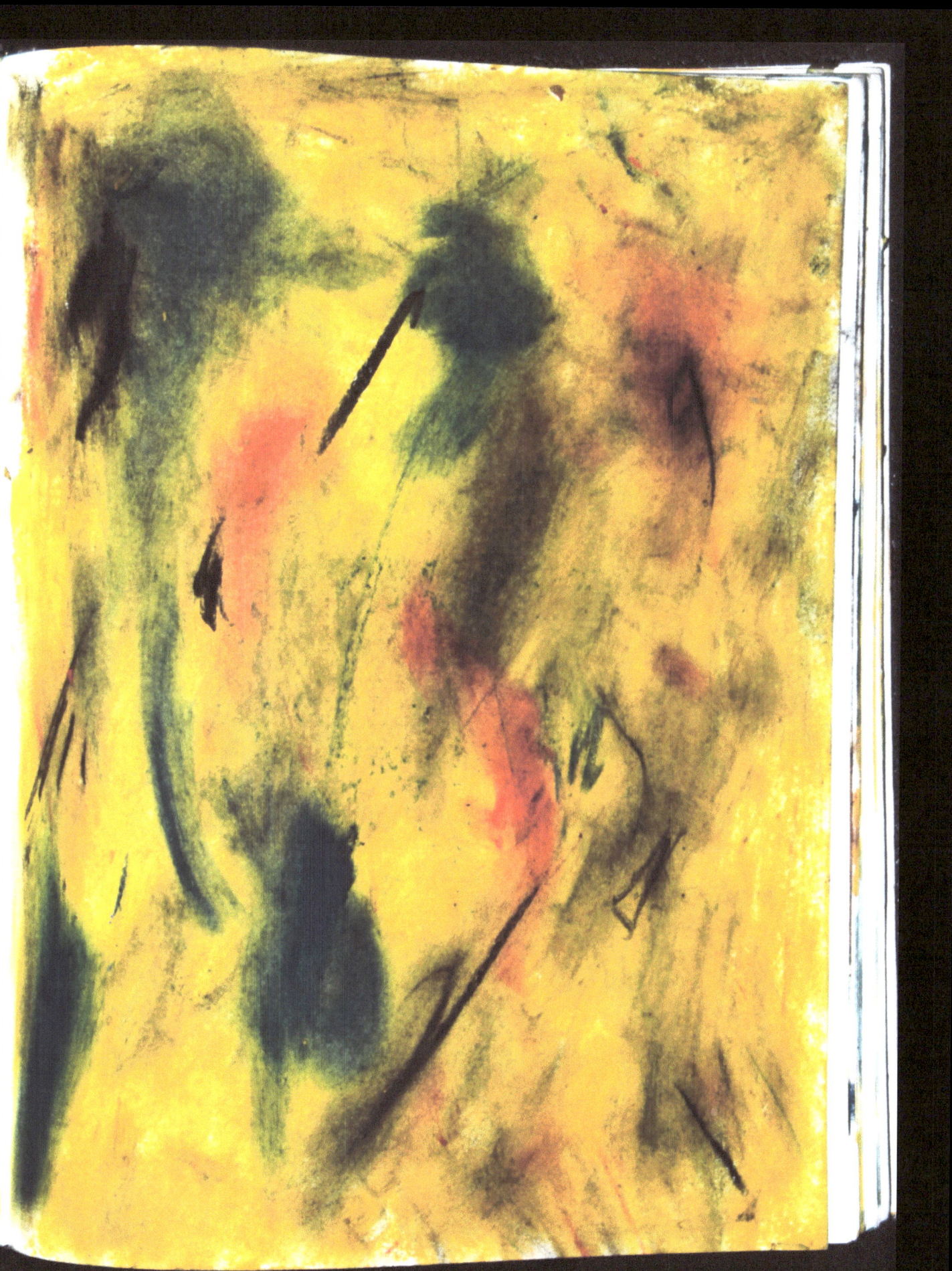

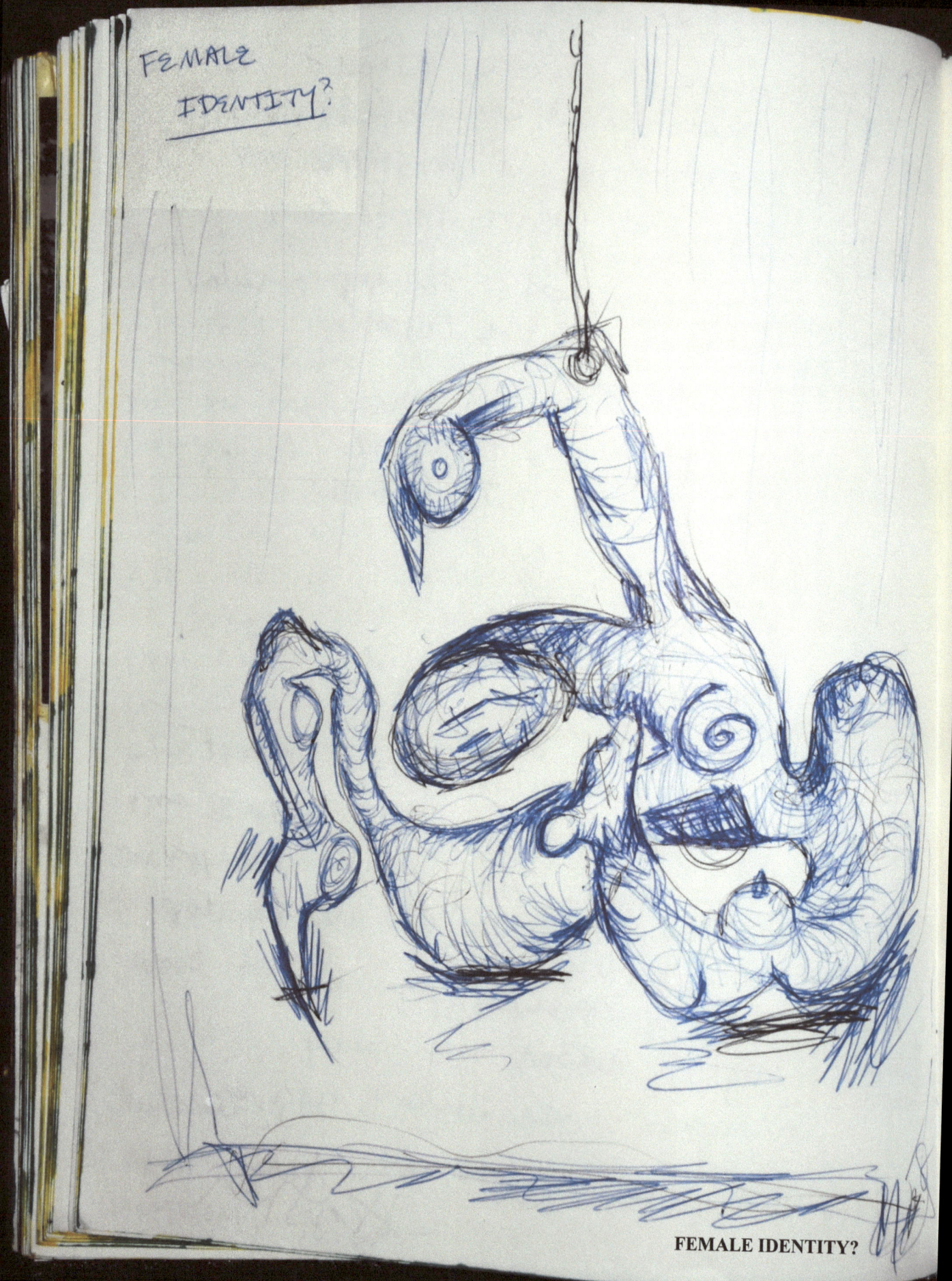

FEMALE
IDENTITY?

FEMALE IDENTITY?

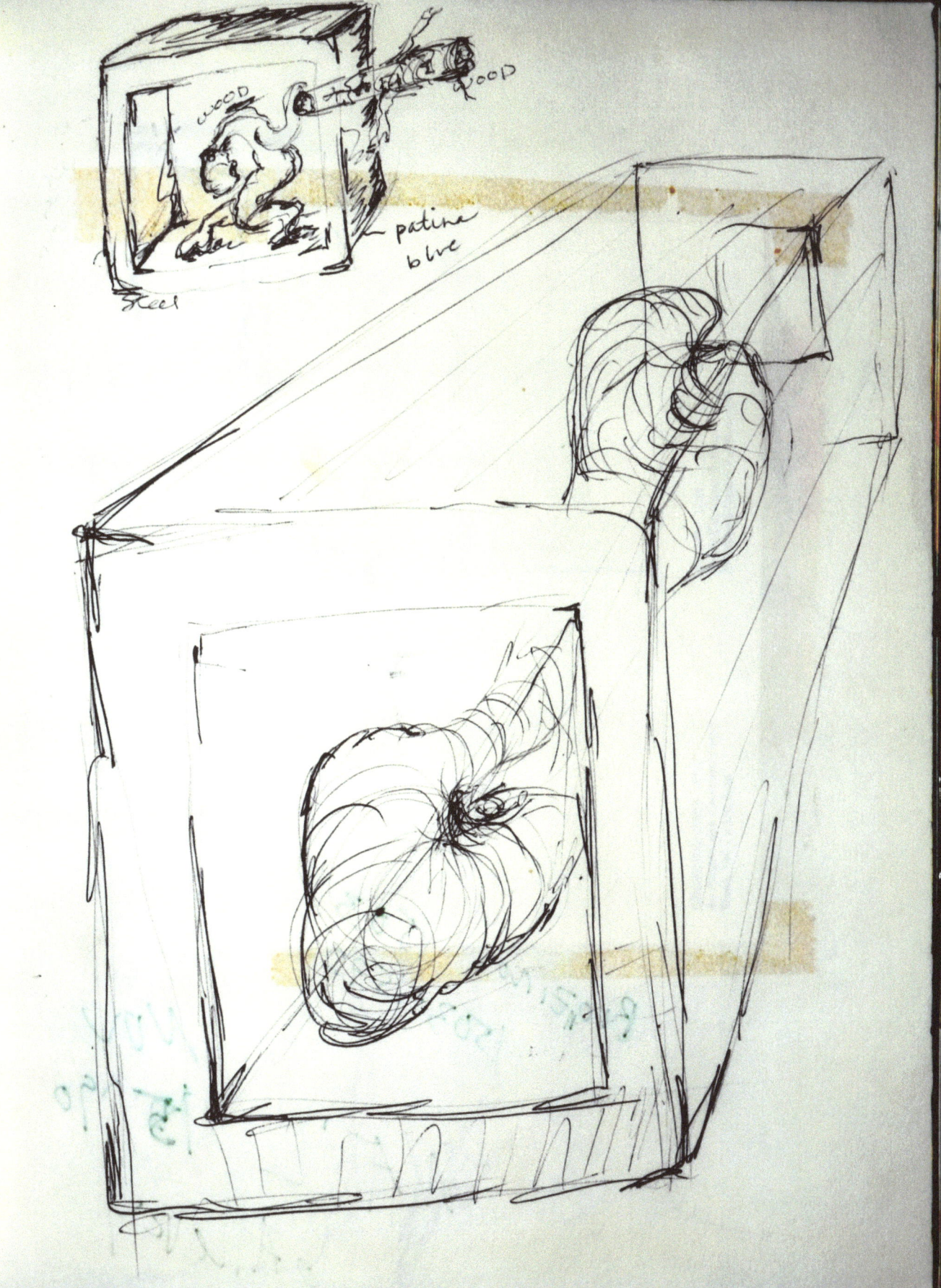

WOOD

WOOD

Steel

patina
blue

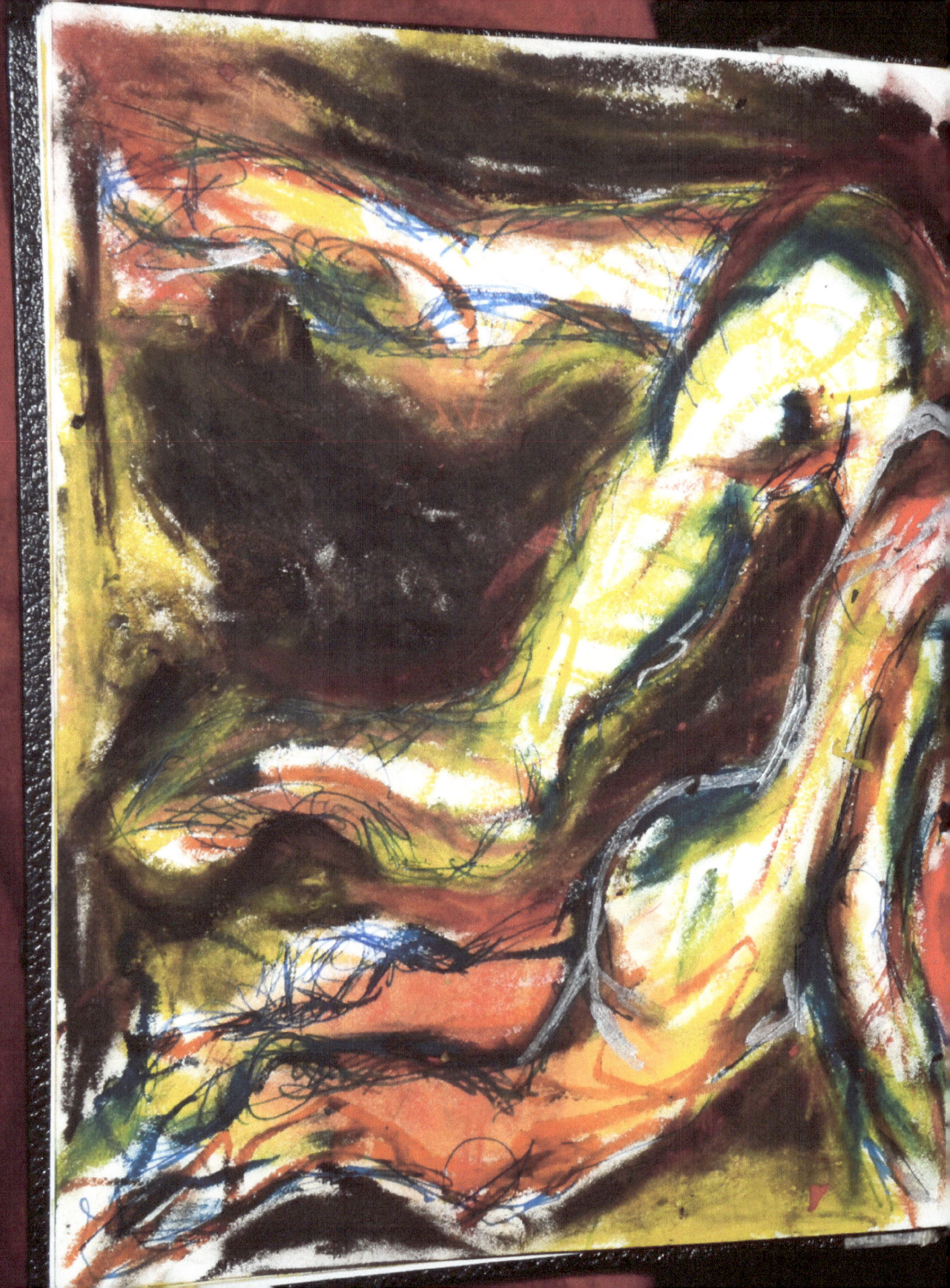

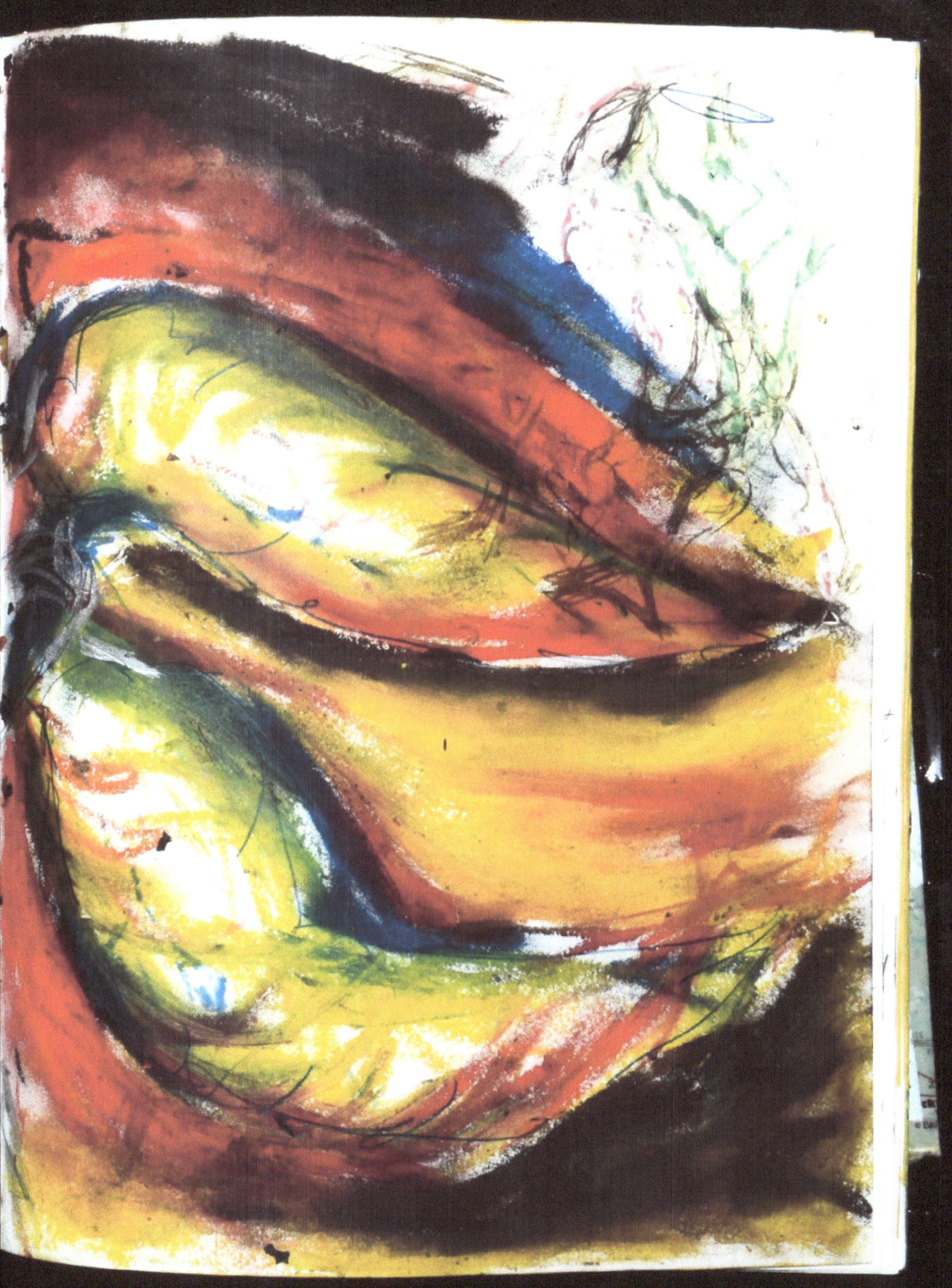

OF MY

chaos

LONDON

CRAZE

THE END

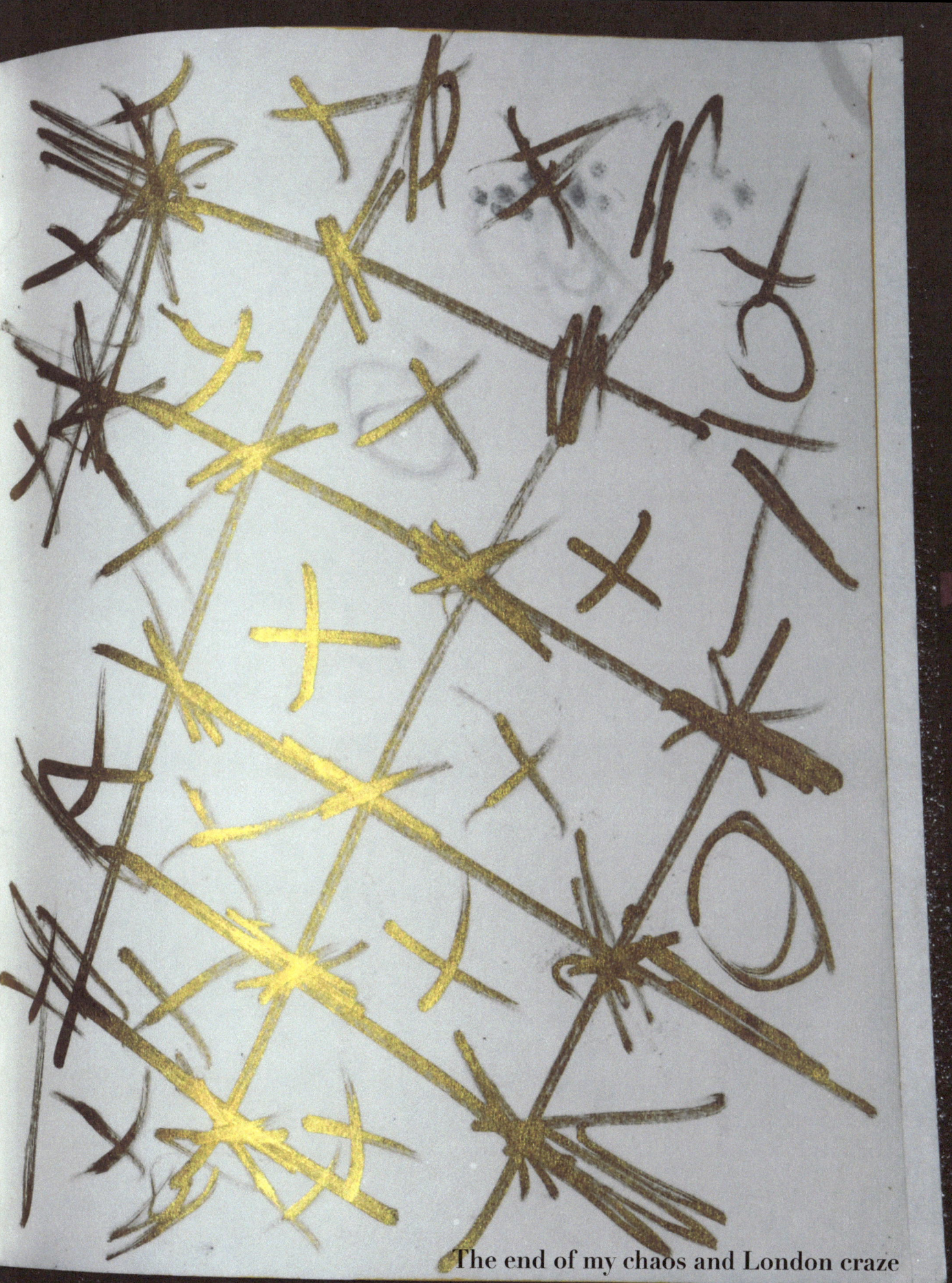

The end of my chaos and London craze

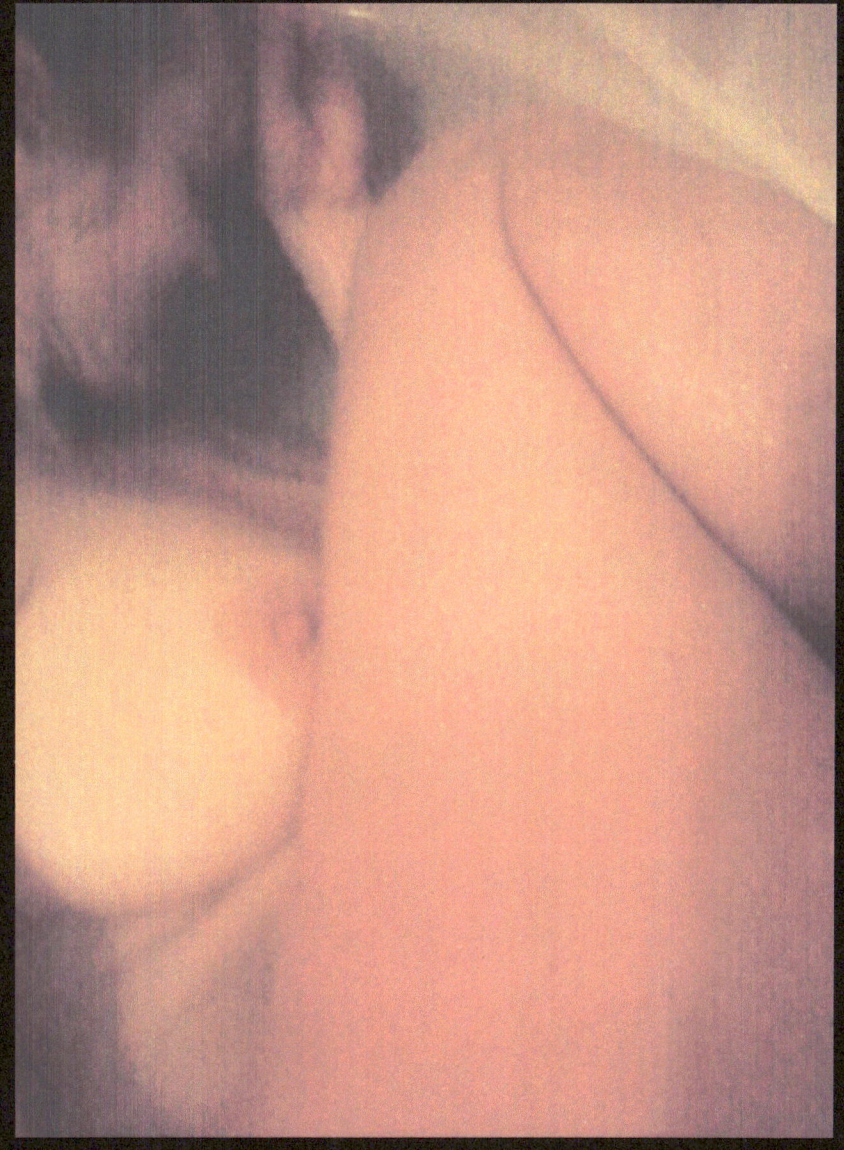

Sophia Leah grew up
in Chicago, Illinois. She received a Bachelor of Science degree in
photography and a minor in sculpture from Syracuse University.
This first journal, Volume #1, was created
while she was a university student studying in
England.

Sophia's next journal, Volume #2, expresses
her angst as an independent young adult
finding her way.